The
Coffee Self-Talk™
Guided Journal

Writing Prompts & Inspiration
for Living Your Magical Life

Kristen Helmstetter

*Green
Butterfly
Press*

The Coffee Self-Talk™ Guided Journal

Copyright © 2021 by Kristen Helmstetter

ISBN: 979-8-9850203-0-4

v1.0

About the Author

In 2018, Kristen Helmstetter sold everything to travel the world with her husband and daughter. She currently lives in a medieval hilltop town in Umbria, Italy. She writes romance novels under the pen name Brisa Starr.

You can find her on Instagram:

instagram.com/coffeeselftalk

Other Books by Kristen Helmstetter

Coffee Self-Talk: 5 Minutes a Day to Start Living Your Magical Life

The Coffee Self-Talk Daily Reader #1: Bite-Sized Nuggets of Magic to Add to Your Morning Routine

Coffee Self-Talk for Dudes: 5 Minutes a Day to Start Living Your Legendary Life

> *Coffee Self-Talk for Dudes* is 95% the same book as *Coffee Self-Talk*, but oriented toward men.

The Coffee Self-Talk Blank Journal (blank with lines)

Coffee Self-Talk for Teen Girls

Coffee Self-Talk for Teen Girls Blank Journal (blank with lines)

Pillow Self-Talk (coming 2021)

Contents

Preface

Hi! My name is Kristen Helmstetter. I'm the author of the book, *Coffee Self-Talk*, which teaches a powerful, five-minute morning ritual to start living your most magical life. It involves taking a mindful moment with your delicious coffee, reading and saying a few beautiful, positive affirmations, and setting up your day for sparkling happiness.

Coffee Self-Talk transforms you by boosting your self-esteem, filling you with joy, creating feelings of wholeness and worthiness, and helping you attract the brilliant, magical life you dream of living. If you are not familiar with the book, *Coffee Self-Talk*, I highly recommend you get it!

I created this companion volume, the *Coffee Self-Talk Guided Journal*, to provide you with activities that will help you draw your dreams to you faster, take action toward reaching your goals, and start living your most magical life, faster.

Whether you want help with your transformation, or you simply want to get to know yourself better, this guided journal will help.

As Mark Twain said,

> *"Throw off the bowlines, sail away from safe harbor,
> catch the trade winds in your sails. Explore, Dream, Discover."*

All my very best and tons of love to you,

Introduction

Welcome to the Coffee Self-Talk Guided Journal.

I'm thrilled to have you here with me for this magical journal experience.

Journaling is about self-discovery—and this journal is perfect for that—but it's also *much* more. This guided journal is designed to help draw your dreams closer to you and start living your magical life, faster. You're about to embark on an exciting journey, in which you'll begin to think and feel really good as you proceed through this book. It's filled with fun exercises, in which you'll do a bit of digging into your psyche to harvest hidden gems, get to know yourself better, inspire yourself, and help you transform into the new you.

This guided journal will help you navigate life's flow with more ease, inspire creativity, reduce stress, and increase your self-love. Don't be surprised if it makes you smile more, too!

There is no right or wrong way to go through the journal. You can start at the beginning and work your way through, or you can open it up to a random spot and see where you land. I highly recommend getting your favorite pens, stickers, and colored pencils, to add as much color, emotion, and fun as possible.

Some entries will be doable in one sitting. Others you might want to chew on a bit before completing them. Any pace you set for yourself is fine.

Your life is waiting for you to shape your destiny. *Let's go!*

I poured love and energy into this private space for growth and reflection that you hold in your hands. As you go through the days, know that I'm right next to you, cheering you on and giving you loud, smacky high-fives. If you have questions along the way, I'm only an email away...

kristen@KristenHelmstetter.com

Or you can reach me on Instagram at:

instagram.com/coffeeselftalk

Don't be shy, reach out! I'd love to hear from you, even if it's just to say *Hi!*

The purpose of our lives is to be happy.

— Dalai Lama

What I Love About My Life...

My life is filled with wonder and awe, and I am powerful.

Take a few minutes, and write about what you love about your life.

For some, this will be easy, with so many things to write about, that you wish there were more pages with lines!

For others, it may be a challenge... if you're going through a difficult time, it can be hard to see the good things around you. But this is always a matter of perspective and choosing to focus—if only for this exercise—on things that you do actually love about your life. The harder this is to do, the more important it is that you do it anyway.

I

The Perfect Day

I love today, because I'm in charge of my day. I make it what I want!

I am life, love, and all things possible.

Imagine you're about to have your perfect day. What would happen? What would you do? Where would you go? Who would you be with? What would you eat? Think through the day, from waking up to going to bed, and write them down as bullets here:

☆

☆

☆

☆

☆

☆

☆

☆

☆

☆

☆

☆

Designing the New You

My life is incredible. I get out and do it! I am a creator.

Today, you're in the factory of your mind, and you're designing the new you. You can transform into anything you want to be. You can live any way you want to live. You're building your dream life *right now*. It's like you're in a factory that makes custom cars, and you get to choose all the specs of your sweet, new ride. Go to town, and have fun. Smile the entire time you answer the questions below. *Enjoy the process!*

Your Turn to Shine!

What do you want out of life?

....

....

....

....

In the new life of your design, what does your typical day look like?

....

....

....

What do you want to do for a career in your new life? (If you're retired, what major projects would you undertake in your new life?)

What are your finances like in your new life? What kind of things will you buy? How much will you have in the bank? Will you invest?

How generous is this new you?

Where does this new you live?

....

What does your house look like?

....

What hobbies does this new you have?

....

....

....

Where does this new you travel?

....

....

Who do you hang out with?

....

....

What does this new you look like?

....

....

Big, Wild Ideas List

I am available for anything that wants to happen in this moment,

including all of the wonderful things beyond my imagination.

Today, you get to make a list of big, wild ideas about what you can do with your life. Hop on the train with me to Innovation Station. Today, we go big!

Literally... no limits today.

For example, when I did this exercise one day, I thought to myself... *maybe I'll manufacture electric cars someday, or maybe I'll invent something for colonizing Mars.* Am I an engineer? Nope. Am I a scientist? Nope. Billionaire hedge fund manager? Not that I know of.

Does this sound crazy? *Hell yes!* That's the whole point! Like... crazy, and big, and weird, and awesome! Does it mean those things are going to actually happen? Not necessarily. Maybe?

So why do it?

Because it gets you thinking big!

There's a saying by Norman Vincent Peale:

Shoot for the moon. Even if you miss, you'll land among the stars.

Most of us are conditioned to expect lives of mediocrity. We were not trained to think big. It's not our *habit*. Or worse, it's seen as a negative thing, like being unrealistic. Or setting ourselves up for disappointment.

Well, to hell with that.

Once I started thinking about manufacturing cars, I started thinking about what kind of cars, what they would look like, and what kind of materials they would be made from. And I ended up thinking about a new kind of cup holder. Because... coffee.

Will I design and manufacture my awesome new cup holder? Maybe not. But if I wanted to explore the idea, there are all kinds of affordable options nowadays for hiring freelance product designers on Fiverr.com, getting 3D-printed prototypes, and even outsourcing manufacturing. With low barriers to entry, and no gatekeepers telling you "no," there's never been a better time to be an entrepreneur.

But that's not the point.

The point is to train your brain to think *without limits*. Anyone can do this, and when you do, ideas come to you *all the time*. Not just about cup holders, but everything in your life. So many ideas that you can ignore 99% of them and cherry-pick only the very best—the ones that excite you most—and run with them. Projects to do, places to travel, things you want to learn, ways to decorate your house... or like I do, books to write.

The trick to coming up with ideas is learning not to judge them. At least, not until later. You want to spurt out as many ideas as you can, all the time. Vet the good ones later. For now, shoot for quantity, not quality. And the more often you repeat today's exercise, the more natural it will become, as you train your brain to become an *idea creation machine*.

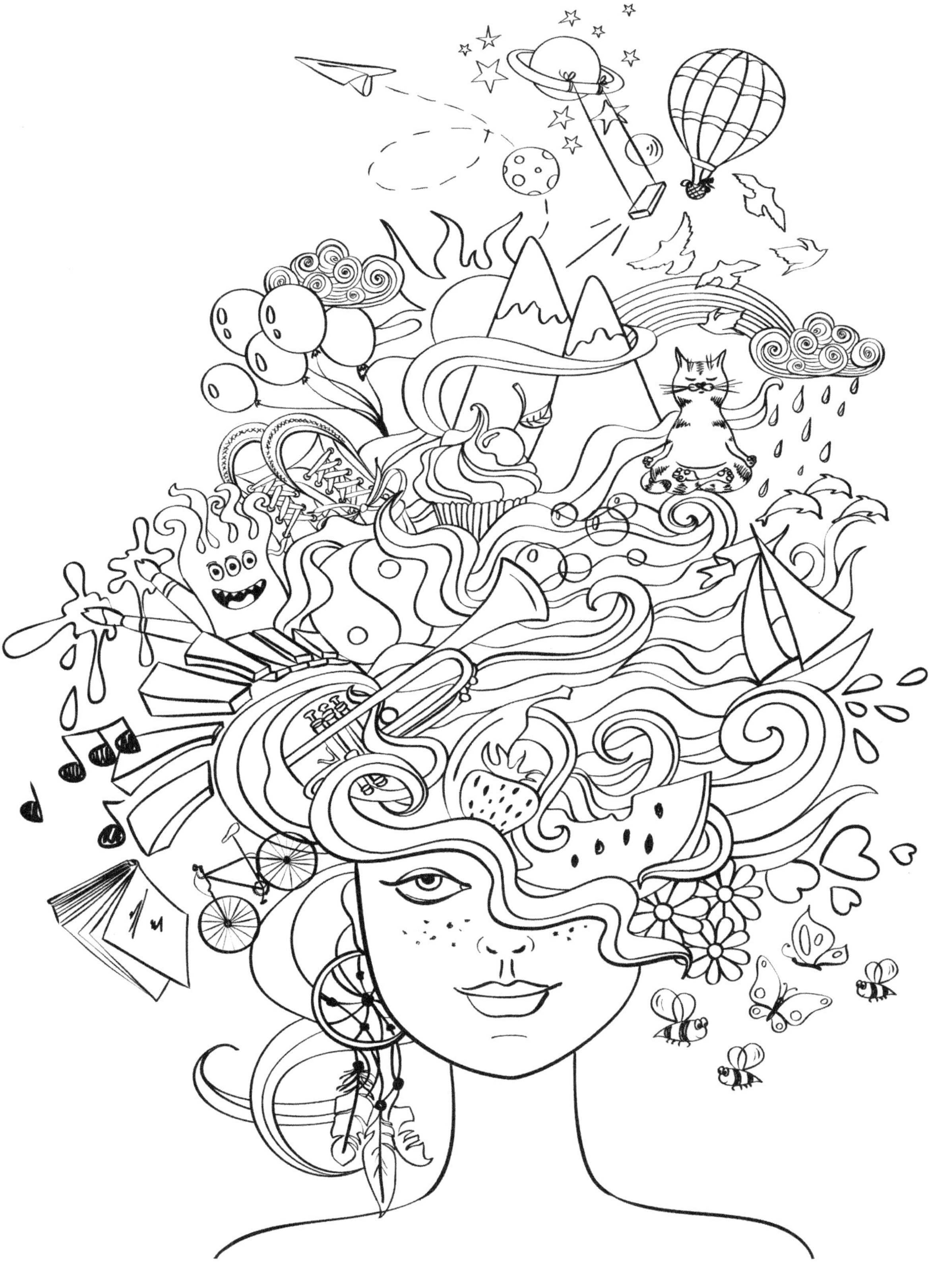

Your Turn to Shine!

Write ten big, wild ideas for hobbies you could try, or businesses you could go into. It doesn't matter how big! Take a couple of minutes and ponder each one, wondering why the idea came to you.

1.

2.

3.

4.

5.

6.

7.

8.

9.

10.

Mood Check-in

I believe in me, right here and right now.

Today is a writing prompt to check in on your mood at the moment.

Today, my mood is....

....

....

Why do you feel the way you do?

....

....

....

....

....

....

Letter of Encouragement

I am living my legendary life, because I can. It is my birthright.

Write a letter of encouragement to yourself about something you're working on, or a goal you're striving for, or a dream you're manifesting. Be your biggest cheerleader, and use this letter to convince yourself how amazing you are, and how you'll power through and manifest everything you desire in your magical life.

Grateful and Why

Let us be grateful to the people who make us happy.

They are the charming gardeners who make our souls blossom.

— Marcel Proust

Being grateful has tons of physical, mental, and spiritual benefits. That's why regularly tapping into this amazing power is life-changing. It has become trendy in self-help circles to periodically (or daily) list things we're grateful for. Which usually means simply listing them, and that's great. But today, let's take things a step further and write down *why* you are grateful for these things. Describing the *why* always takes your thinking to a deeper level, and helps you appreciate them even more.

I have my daughter tell me something she's grateful about every few days. She sends me her "grateful and why" list via text message. It always makes me smile (and chuckle) at some of the amazing reasons she's grateful for something.

Your Turn to Shine!

List five things you're grateful for now, and for each one, write two reasons why.

1. I am grateful for ....

     Reason #1 ....

     Reason #2 ....

2. I am grateful for

    Reason #1

    Reason #2

3. I am grateful for

    Reason #1

    Reason #2

4. I am grateful for

    Reason #1

    Reason #2

5. I am grateful for

    Reason #1

    Reason #2

Magical Mind Wandering

My imagination,

aroused emotionally to a crazy-intense degree of excitement,

plus my confident expectancy,

bring an avalanche of sparkling fortune to me.

Today is a beautiful day for *Magical Mind Wandering*. That's when you let your mind wander, without guardrails or restrictions. You get to go on a fantastic journey that's fun in the moment while you're thinking about these things, but also useful as you imagine the magical life you want to live and manifest.

Today's exercise will be helpful in opening your mind.

Your Turn to Shine!

What is your favorite season, and why?

....

....

What is your favorite kind of weather, and why?

....

....

What is a place that inspires you, and why?

Look around where you're sitting. What are five colorful or beautiful things that you can see right now?

What are three places you would like to visit, and why?

Who are three public figures or celebrities (alive) who inspire you, and why?

What is something you use daily that you are grateful was invented?

What is your favorite meal or dish? And what is your favorite dessert?

What is something that excites you?

What is one thing that makes your life easier?

What is one subject you know a lot about?

What is one thing you're more skilled at now than you used to be? How did you get better at it?

If you could do one thing you can't do today, what would it be, and why?

_____

_____

What is one thing that is going well in your life right now?

_____

_____

What are three things you've never done, but you'd love to try?

_____

_____

_____

What is something you can do to move toward making one of these things happen?

_____

_____

_____

Diving into Dreams

I feel amazing, and I have an incredible life of vitality and bliss.

Do you have any recurring dreams? If so, describe it here.

If you don't have any recurring dreams, then describe a dream that you remember as being particularly vivid. Does the dream hold any significance for you? If so, what? How does the dream make you feel?

Imagination Station

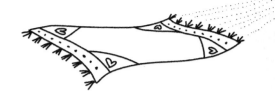

I feel like I'm on a scarlet magic carpet ride,

soaring through a star-bursting sky, filled with awe and wonder.

Einstein said, *"The true sign of intelligence is not knowledge, but imagination."*

Let's take a ride to Imagination Station. In this place, everybody uses their glittery imagination to live and create. There are no blockages. There are no judgments. It is *pure imagination,* and you come here to let yourself go, open your mind, and let it play in a field of wildflowers.

For the next ten minutes, at Imagination Station, anything can happen, from dragons and dinosaurs, to kitchen faucets that pour champagne. You're going to write down anything that comes from your imagination. Anything creative, or any story you've ever thought of. Any crazy idea you've ever had. Any question you've ever asked. Any dream you've dared not to dream.

I know there are things that pop into our heads at random times, but they get promptly squashed by our judging mind, or by the distraction of life's many to-do's. Today, you have the freedom to explore your imagination and follow whatever pops into it, whether practical, goofy, or magical. See how far you can take it!

Your Turn to Shine!

Set your alarm for ten minutes, and write everything that comes into your mind while you visit Imagination Station. Enjoy your ride!

Happiness Touchstones

I'm unstoppable because I know that anything is possible.

I'm ready to dive into my day with gusto,

and I am having the most amazing time! I love my life!

Happiness touchstones are the little things that bring happiness to your life. When you see them, or taste them, or smell them, or hear them, you get a warm, feathery-soft feeling that goes through you. These things are enjoyable. For me, my list would include things like river rocks worn smooth, willow trees with soft grass underneath, rose bushes in full bloom, black coffee, colorful buildings, cobblestone streets in Italy, crystal quartz, my daughter's hands, the smell of jasmine. Um... bacon.

What about you? Today, you get to make a list of happiness touchstones.

Your Turn to Shine!

Write a list of the little things you love, your happiness touchstones. Draw a picture of one of the items. Or acquire it, and take a photo.

1. ....

2. ....

3. ....

4. ....

5. ....

6. ....

7. ....

8. ....

9. ....

10. ....

If you draw a picture, do it here:

Love Letter to Me

My thankful heart is always close to the riches of the universe.

I am grateful for my beautiful life and my success.

My life is magical.

Write yourself a love letter, and pour your heart out to yourself, telling yourself all of the reasons why you love yourself so much. (If this is difficult, then be sure to add some self-love lines to your daily Coffee Self-Talk script.)

Rapid-Fire Fun

I stand in my own power at all times.

The purpose of this exercise is to have fun and get to know yourself better. Write the first thing that comes to mind as you go through these questions. Don't overthink or spend time processing or ranking possible alternatives.

For even more fun, ask these questions to your kids, or your significant other, and share your answers! You could do this around the dinner table, for instance. Or make a game of it, using your phone's stopwatch and a five or ten-second time limit, to really force people to say the first thing that comes to mind.

Your Turn to Shine!

What is your favorite thing to do by yourself?

What is your favorite thing to do with friends?

What are you excited about today?

What are you excited about this year?

What's your favorite thing to do on your birthday?

If you could be any animal for a day, which one would you be, and why?

What makes you laugh?

What sounds do you hear right now?

Which fictional character would you most like to meet?

What is your favorite scent?

What is your favorite sport to play?

What is your favorite sport to watch?

When do you feel peaceful and chill?

What is the best thing about your life right now?

What was/is your favorite subject in school?

What song makes you feel good?

What do you love to talk about?

If you had $100 to spend on anything (but not paying bills), what would you do/buy?

Magical Life Haiku

I feel amazing and have an incredible life, full of peace and bliss.

Haiku is a form of Japanese poetry that is short, usually unrhymed, usually evokes natural imagery or the seasons, and examines a single moment in time.

Here's the structure of a haiku:

First line: 5 syllables

Second line: 7 syllables

Third line: 5 syllables

Here's an example of a haiku, written by poet Laura Lee Bond, author of *The Love Around Us: Some Haiku-Inspired Essays to Brighten Your Day:*

> *a snowflake melted*
>
> *on my lip it tasted of*
>
> *lonely solitude*

The first time I wrote a haiku, it intimidated me, but it turned out to be so fun. Now I want to write them all the time. It's a great way to be creative and make connections in your mind about living a magical life, full of sensory images and experiences.

Using the 5-7-5 structure described above, here is the first haiku I wrote. (It breaks the guidelines by rhyming a bit, but I just didn't resonate with any other words I tried, so I left it the way it first came to my mind.)

Happiness is mine,

warm sunny flowers are born.

Sparkle shimmer shine.

Your Turn to Shine!

It's time to write a haiku. Roll up your haiku sleeves and dive in. Have fun, and just go with it. Write whatever comes to mind, and try different lines until you come up with what you want. Keep it simple. There's no need to attempt flowery language. Capitalization and punctuation are optional... do whatever you want.

Today's subject for your haiku: *Living your magical life.*

This is a beautiful opportunity to look around and pay attention to the small details of living your magical, day-to-day life. You could start with something that's visually beautiful, or warm, or cozy, or it could be an uplifted emotion... happiness, growth, abundance, health, awe, love.

Use your senses. What do you hear, taste, feel, see, smell?

What season does it evoke?

Is there an object or symbol involved? Your dog? A warm blanket? A butterfly? A mountain? A flower? Self-talk? Honey? Wine? The beach?

Or... *coffee?*

Use short phrases that evoke potent emotional images. Remember, 5-7-5 syllables. And feel free to write as many haiku as you'd like!

Write It 50 Times

I am calm, because I am confident and self-assured.

I am worthy of all of my heart's desires.

love
love
love
love
love
love

When I was young, and I'd get in trouble, my mom would make me write a sentence 50 times. The sentence was usually something like, *I will not break my brother's toys.* Or, *I will be nice to my brother.* Or, *I love my brother.*

Don't feel bad for him, he had to write his own 50 lines about me!

It reminds me of the opening to *The Simpsons*, when Bart writes something funny on the chalkboard for each new episode...

I will not sell land in Florida.

I will not hide behind the Fifth Amendment.

I will not eat things for money.

I realize my mom made me do this to teach me a lesson, and that it was a consequence of bad behavior, but the idea is also a great tool for reinforcing *good* behavior. That's because the mind is always listening to everything you say and think.

So, even if I had to write something repeatedly as a result of doing something wrong, the writing still had a positive effect. After all, I love my brother so much... it worked! *Hehe.*

Today's writing is about self-love.

Many people struggle with self-love, and the simple exercise below will infuse powerful words deeper into your mind and heart. Even if you feel fake while writing it, don't worry... it will still have a positive effect.

Your Turn to Shine!

Write each of the following five affirmations ten times (for a total of 50). The repetition will help wire them permanently into your brain.

- *I am amazing!*

- *I feel fabulous!*

- *I love my life!*

- *I am worthy of my dreams!*

- *Life loves me!*

Make it more fun by doing each group in a different color pen or writing style. Add stars and hearts for extra manifesting mojo!

If you find yourself zoning out while doing it, or thinking about other things, then bring your focus back to the words. Saying them out loud as you write them will help. And this exercise will be extra powerful if you also tap into an uplifting emotion while writing them. Conjure up some *awe,* or *generosity,* or *love,* or *gratitude* while writing them.

Have fun!

I am amazing!

_____   _____

_____   _____

_____   _____

_____   _____

_____   _____

I feel fabulous!

_____   _____

_____   _____

_____   _____

_____   _____

_____   _____

I love my life!

_____   _____

_____   _____

_____   _____

_____   _____

_____   _____

I am worthy of my dreams!

Life loves me!

Your Favorite Part of the Day

Great things happen to those who don't stop believing,

trying, learning, and being grateful.

— Roy T. Bennett

Being grateful can be as simple as thinking about something that is a favorite of yours. Today's activity is going to focus on a part of your day you enjoy the most. And you're going to dig into why it is a favorite part of your day.

You'll feel gratitude while doing the exercise because you get to think and feel about this time you enjoy. But it also serves to get you thinking about how you can have this experience more often.

For example, my favorite part of the day is when I wake up in the morning. I absolutely love my first two cups of coffee. I love the magical silence in the house at this time, and I love doing my Coffee Self-Talk. By recognizing how much I adore this special time, it suggests I might look for other times in the day where I can create a similar scenario.

Your Turn to Shine!

What is your favorite part of the day?

What do you do during this part of your day?

_____

_____

_____

Are there other people around? If so, who?

_____

_____

_____

How do you feel during this time?

_____

_____

_____

Is there another time during the day when you can duplicate this experience?

_____

Take a moment, and feel gratitude for this part of the day... close your eyes, imagine it, and feel how much you love it.

Magical Manifesting Sauce

By feeling and practicing gratitude in your waking day,

you're in a state to receive. You are in an energy

that is drawing something to you on a moment-to-moment basis.

— Dr. Joe Dispenza

Did you know you can train your brain to be grateful for the little things in life? You can.

Why would you want to do this? Because, this way, you can have a non-stop drip of feel-goodness going through you. All. The. Time.

It's like an IV drip of happiness!

You see, when you feel gratitude, your brain gets flooded with brain chemicals (dopamine and serotonin) that make you feel good. It's a natural high, and it motivates you to want to feel it over and over. It's addictive, in a good way!

Feeling gratitude has incredible benefits for your body and brain, and it helps you attract your dreams and goals to you faster. According to the *UCLA Mindfulness Awareness Research Center*, regularly expressing gratitude changes the structure of your brain. (Wow!) It keeps the gray matter functioning, and you become healthier and happier.

- Grateful people feel better and healthier. *Longevity, yes!*

- Mental health is improved with gratitude. *It reduces depression and blood pressure, yay!*

- You sleep better with gratitude. *Yippee! Deep sleep and dreams, here I come!*

- Gratitude reduces stress dramatically. *Woohoo!*

- Gratitude will make you more satisfied with your life. *Life is awesome!*

No matter what's going on in your life, you'll have more *grit and resilience* with gratitude.

In an interview on *The Next Big Idea Club*, Caren Baruch-Feldman (a clinical psychologist who works on developing grit and self-control) said,

"When you're grateful, you're focusing on what is working, what is positive, what is good in your life. That decreases stress, and lets you be more optimistic and more positive, which are things you need to be in terms of being resilient and persistent.

"I often talk about this experiment that I do, where I ask the audience to try to find the red objects in the room. And then I ask them, what did they see that was blue? Obviously, they can't tell me anything blue, because I told them to look for red. But the point is, what we look for becomes prominent in our life."

Makes sense, right?

When you focus on what you're grateful about, you know… all those things that are going well in your life, or that you appreciate… it makes you feel more positive and fills you with uplifted emotions, and you're more likely to notice the opportunities that are always all around you, but impossible to see when you're mired in negative thinking.

Caren Baruch-Feldman goes on to describe how gratitude relates to grit, and the art of sticking with something, like a project or goal. She said that, when gratitude is the lens you use to view life, this increases your optimism, which is needed for resilience. The gratitude lens allows you to see all the things that are working well in your life.

That's why gratitude is a *magical manifesting sauce*.

We can't feel crappy and great at the same time. It's impossible. As a result of tapping into your gratitude (an elevated emotion), you're instantly transitioning out of any limited emotions, such as fear, anxiety, frustration, or angst. *Boom!* You instantly have more clarity. You see more opportunities. You resonate with other positive and generous people. That's how you manifest your dreams and desires faster!

You're in the frame of mind that's necessary to make shit happen!

When you feel gratitude, you feel abundance right then and there, and when you *feel* abundance, *you attract abundance!*

I take advantage of this neuro-hack every chance I get.

I have entire *gratitude days* where, literally, my whole focus for the day is gratitude, like a non-stop, gushing waterfall of gratitude. A gratitude *marathon*. With every step I take, I think and say things I'm grateful for. For example: Bed. Floor. Toilet. Teeth. Brush. Coffee. Food. Car. Legs. Coffee. Life. Stars. Sunshine. Flowers. Desk. Coffee. Laptop. Trees. Squirrels. Maple scones with icing. Gravity. Coffee. Fireplaces. Microwave ovens. Dental floss.

I could go on and on... *and I do!*

It sounds a little nutty taking it to this extreme, but it's actually *really fun!*

And I double down on my gratitude practice, speaking a constant monologue of these things, out loud whenever possible. If I can't say it out loud, then I at least mouth it.

Every day I spend like this, life gets *bigger!* Then, something will happen, and my heart will burst with gratitude unexpectedly. It'll be so powerful, it makes me stop what I'm doing as I feel enveloped in a magic sauce that's like a warm, sparkly blanket. Like an empowering and sweet, generous hug from the Universe, from myself, from life. And a profound sense of connection washes through me. These are some of the most powerful moments in my life, and the feelings give me overwhelming confidence that my dreams are coming true.

Your Turn to Shine!

Set a timer for two minutes and start a list of things for which you're grateful. Write down every single thing that comes to your mind, no matter how big or small (bed, toilet paper, air conditioning, coffee!). List, list, list. Non-stop write, write, write.

Ready! Set! Go!

Favorite Body Moves

My strength is unlimited because I am full of warm, glowing energy.

It comes from within and expands outside of myself.

My energy is so uplifting and high, that I heal myself with it,

and I also have the power to heal others with it.

Movement and exercise are so important, but people often don't make time for it, or they think they don't like it. I mean, it's not that people don't like moving, but if you're my mom, then you think of exercise as a famous four-letter word. And that word ain't *love*.

But there's a great way to inspire yourself to *move more* every day.

For starters, you want to find things you enjoy doing. And what better way to do that then to make a list, which is what you'll do today.

For example, stretching feels good, and dancing is fun. Both are great ways to move your body. Maybe it's going on a walk, cooking, or playing with your dog. Or maybe it's cleaning. Haha, ok, perhaps you don't enjoy cleaning, but when you realize that cleaning is also a way that your body moves, you realize you're getting two for the price of one.

Why is movement so important?

Moving more is correlated with better memory, improved brain function, and reduced likelihood of depression. Movement can also stimulate happy chemicals inside you. Movement can increase your creativity and help you solve problems. In fact, going for a walk is one of my favorite ways to "work on" my books. I have so much more creativity when I'm walking, especially when it's outside in nature. These are all components of living a magical life.

Your Turn to Shine!

List your ten favorite ways to move your body. After each, write why you like it so much.

1. Movement type ....

   Reason ....

2. Movement type ....

   Reason ....

3. Movement type ....

   Reason ....

4. Movement type ....

   Reason ....

5. Movement type ....

   Reason ....

6. Movement type ....

    Reason ....

7. Movement type ....

    Reason ....

8. Movement type ....

    Reason ....

9. Movement type ....

    Reason ....

10. Movement type ....

    Reason ....

Lofty Questions

I'm tapping into good feelings right now, because that's the key to success.

Today is a fabulous day for asking *lofty questions,* which I first learned about in a video with *Mindvalley's* Vishen Lakhiani. Lofty questions are cool. They're uplifting questions you ask, and answer, about yourself. And they're a clever mental trick, because they presuppose something positive about you. For example:

Why am I always so happy?

See how this presupposes that I'm always happy?

Lofty questions can be about the future self you want to become (or things you want to do or have), typically asked with the word *Why.* This suggests it's already happening, giving you a taste of the future that you desire. And the answer is like a confirmation that it's happening. It's a fun exercise. I even include a few lofty questions in my personal Coffee Self-Talk scripts.

Why Are Lofty Questions Fun and Helpful?

Lofty questions make you more confident and help you manifest your dreams. They help you create answers that stealthily slip in positive manifestation talk. The answers "prove" you're right.

The first time I tried this, I was like, whoa... that's cool! Something shifted in my energy, my brain sat up to attention, and a little smirk played on my lips.

Examples of Lofty Questions I Ask Myself:

Why do I have the vibrant energy of a 25-year-old?

Why does money come to me so easily?

Why do my goals and dreams always manifest so quickly?

Why is it so easy for me to learn Italian?

Why do I have such a powerful memory?

Why is my life so amazing?

Why do I love myself so much?

Why am I so healthy?

Why am I so closely connected to the Universe?

Your Turn to Shine!

Write five lofty questions of your own (or use some of those supplied above). Then, answer those questions.

Question #1

Answer

Question #2

Answer

Question #3

Answer

Question #4

Answer

Question #5

Answer

Looking Forward to...

The future belongs to those who

believe in the beauty of their dreams.

— Eleanor Roosevelt

When you look forward to something, you're optimistic, and studies have shown that optimism is good for us. Optimists have better mental health, and they live longer, too. It makes sense!

Take today to have fun and bask in optimism about your future. Pump that happy muscle, make it stronger by being happy and optimistic. Write about some things you're looking forward to. It could be dinner tonight, a TV show, a specific day that's coming up, or a holiday that's coming up, or a trip somewhere. It could even be that you're looking forward to the transformational process with your Coffee Self-Talk and this journal!

Your Turn to Shine!

Later today, I am looking forward to...

Next week, I am looking forward to...

Next month, I am looking forward to...

Next year, I am looking forward to...

Clear the Cobwebs

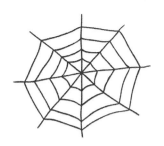

I am freakin' amazing. Right here, right now. Yesssssss!

Today is a day for clearing out the cobwebs. Fill the following pages with anything that's been on your mind lately. Now you have a place to put it, and you don't need to think about it more, unless you want to.

There are no judgments, no right or wrong. No good or bad. Literally, you can write anything you want... your to-do list for the day or month, venting about anxieties, recalling your happiest memory, or a dream you had last night... anything that is in your mind as you write.

Doing this can be like a mini-therapy session, clearing the gunky cobwebs out of your brain, cleaning up, sweeping things out to give you a lovely, beautiful, and clear head for the rest of the day. Or, you may find that the writing process itself stimulates creativity, new thinking, and new ideas.

Whatever you start to write, just go with it, and see where it leads!

Magical Life Vision Board - Part I

It's the moment now, I feel it in my bones,

my blood is singing with my soul...

Let's do this! I rock!

Today's task is to begin planning your vision board (if you don't already have one). Vision boards are popular. And they're fun... you get to see—*in pictures!*—your dreams and goals, and all the wonderful things you'd like to become, have, and do.

Our brains love images. It's one reason I recommend adding images to your Coffee Self-Talk scripts. The extra flair is effective in helping to keep your dreams and goals front and center in your mind. More neurons firing and wiring, and attracting your dream life faster.

Traditional Vision Board

Traditional vision boards, like the ones my husband and I made a decade ago, comprise a cork bulletin board, push-pins or thumbtacks, and pictures we cut out of magazines or printed out on a color printer from images obtained online.

You can hang your board on the wall right by your desk, so you always see it. My vision board was bright, with colors and images that never failed to attract my gaze whenever I walked by.

Or you might want to put your vision board in your bedroom. This way, it's the first thing you see upon waking, and the last thing you see before falling asleep.

Note: Kids love these, too. What a great way to train their brains for happiness and success!

Your Turn to Shine!

If you don't possess the items to create your *Magical Life Vision Board* yet, then order them online, or make a note to pick them up at a local store. In the meantime, or if you already have the necessary items, the next step is to brainstorm, writing down possible pictures you'd like to add to your vision board. The following categories are just suggestions to get you started; feel free to modify however you like.

It's fine to list more ideas than you'll actually add to your board, so cast a wide net now, think out of the box, and you can always narrow your focus later. This is just a place to have fun and play with ideas. And of course, as you're looking for images, you're likely to find some great ones that you had not even been looking for.

Goal Pictures (short and long-term)

Self-Improvement & Spirituality Pictures

Health & Fitness Pictures

....

....

....

Home & Lifestyle Pictures

....

....

....

Family & Relationship Pictures

....

....

....

Nature Pictures

....

....

....

Activities & Hobbies Pictures

_____   _____

_____   _____

_____   _____

Travel Pictures

_____   _____

_____   _____

_____   _____

Career Pictures

_____   _____

_____   _____

_____   _____

Purchases & Physical Objects Pictures

_____   _____

_____   _____

_____   _____

Skills Pictures

_____   _____

_____   _____

_____   _____

Finances & Investing Pictures

_____   _____

_____   _____

_____   _____

Other Pictures

_____   _____

_____   _____

_____   _____

Magical Life Vision Board
Part II - *Mobile Board!*

In the previous exercise, you planned your *Magical Life Vision Board*, and we assumed it would be a physical board with pictures you stick to it.

Today, we're going to discuss how to make a mobile version of your vision board on your phone!

There's no writing exercise today. Instead, I'm going to provide you with step-by-step instructions for creating your mobile vision board, and then you can fill it with pictures you download from the internet, based on the ideas you wrote down in the previous day's exercise.

Note: Shout out to my beautiful, high-vibe friend Elizabeth (ElizabethPayne.com) for this great idea. The specific steps for using the software described below may differ slightly between phones, or as the app updates with newer versions, but the general concept should still apply.

Step 1. Get Your Phone's Screen Size

Open your web browser, and search on your phone's model + the words "screen size." The results should come up with a size in pixels. For example, the iPhone 11 Pro Max is 2688 × 1242 pixels. The iPhone 11 is 1792 × 828 pixels. Write down your phone's size in pixels.

Step 2. Download Canva App

Go to your phone's app store, and download the "Canva" app (there's a free version). The app is called *Canva: Graphic Design & Video.*

Step 3. Create a Design

Open the Canva app, and on the homepage, tap the "+" in the bottom right-hand corner of the screen. Choose "+ Custom size." Enter the pixel size from Step 1. Enter the smaller number for the width, and the large number for the height. Confirm it says "px" beside the input boxes. Tap the "Create new design" button.

Step 4. Add the Picture Grid

In the Canva app, on the menu bar, select "Elements." Scroll down to "Grids" and tap "See all." Select the desired layout for your vision board.

Step 5. Uploading Pictures

Tap the "+" icon at the bottom of the screen. Choose "Uploads." Tap the "Upload media" button at the top. Choose your image location. Navigate to and select the images, and tap "Add." You can choose more than one image to upload at a time. Repeat until all images are uploaded.

Step 6. Add Pictures to Design

Make sure you are still on the "Uploads" tab. Tap on the picture you want to add. The picture will appear in the middle of the design. Tap and drag the picture to the desired location on the grid. To adjust the picture inside the grid, double tap on the picture and adjust to desired size. Repeat the steps for each section of the grid.

Step 7. Optional Adjustment

If you want to adjust the overall size of the grids, tap once on the design. Use the handles on the sides or corners to adjust.

Step 8. Download/Publish

After you have completed your masterpiece, tap the "Upload" icon in the top-right corner of your screen. Tap "Save as..." and then the "Download" button to save the image to your phone. Now you can open your photos and see this anytime, or make it your lock-screen.

Congratulations!

You now have a mobile version of your *Magical Life Vision Board!*

Body Love

Walk as if you are kissing the Earth with your feet.

— Thich Nhat Hanh

Having a healthy self-image and loving your body is of paramount importance for living your magical life. Too many people criticize their body on a daily, and even hourly, basis. Not enough people take the time to feel gratitude for their amazing body, because they're always wanting to change it. If that's you, that ends here and now.

The important thing to know is that, when you want to change your body, whether to be a different size or shape, or to be healthier, or stronger, the foundation starts with self-love for your *current* body. I'll repeat... it *starts with self-love.*

Why?

Because this helps you make the changes you desire faster!

It starts with looking in the mirror and saying to your body, *I love you the way you are.* This helps you to relax, which allows your body to change and heal faster. It starts with looking at whatever part you usually criticize, whether it is your hands, or your legs, or your nose, and telling those parts how much you love *and appreciate* them.

Kiss the body part, if you can.

And if you're one of those people who jokes about your body, to "deal" with it, then stop it. Your body wants and deserves love. You deserve love. So give it to yourself.

Sometimes, it's hard to tell something that you've spent so much time criticizing that you love it. One way to start is by simply telling your body that *you appreciate it,* every day. Over time, this will turn into a stronger love, which will turn into a healthy self-image. This does not mean you don't have goals for your body, but the goals are *way* easier to attain when you start from a place of love.

It's simply magical the way it works. In fact, everything in your life will get better and easier when you have a healthy self-image. *Everything!*

The curious paradox is that,

when I accept myself just as I am, then I change.

— Carl Rogers

So, even if you feel like it's insincere at the start, keep at it, keep telling all those parts of your body (and your body as a whole) how much you appreciate it, giving gratitude for it. You can give gratitude for the parts that you truly do love right now, to get the love ball rolling.

Your life will change, I promise.

Your Turn to Shine!

On the following page, write your body a love letter. If you need some prompts to get you going, tell your body what you love about it, describe your gratitude for the whole of it, and then the specific parts. Start at the top, with your hair and head, and work your way down until you get to the tips of your toes. Think of a list of loving words to help you. Think of your body from both the inside (the cells, tissues, muscle, bones, joints, organs), as well as the outside (skin and shape).

Dear Body,

Your Explorer's List

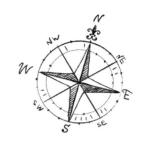

I have an amazing brain, heart, and soul.

I am capable of accomplishing whatever I set out to do.

I am limitless.

Living a magical life includes constantly exploring new territories, taking chances, and going places you've never been before. Today, you'll make an exciting list by diving into this idea. Think of places to go, foods to taste, hobbies to try, chances to take, classes to sign up for, businesses to start. Put on your Magellan hat, and see where the wind and currents take you!

Your Turn to Shine!

What are five things you can do to explore your incredible life more? Is there a way you can take a chance on something or someone? Are there places, nearby or far, that you can explore today, or in the near future?

For each thing you list, also write the compelling *why* that fires in your heart and makes you want to explore it.

Exploration #1

Why?

Exploration #2

Why?

Exploration #3

Why?

Exploration #4

Why?

Exploration #5

Why?

Your Golden Intuition

My inner voice possesses wisdom and experience,

and I listen to what it tells me.

Feel your intuition.

Honor your intuition.

Let it guide you.

Intuition is a big part of my life. You know, that gut feeling.

I first learned about intuition when I was in a relationship that wasn't healthy. My mom asked me one day, *"Are there any red flags?"* That was another way of asking, *"What does your gut tell you? Are there things that don't feel right?"*

That discussion didn't happen until my early 20s. I wish I had known more about following my intuition, or listening to the feeling in my gut, when I was younger. Intuition is important. And it's *vital* for living a magical life.

To Intuit or Not to Intuit

Sometimes, bad things are obvious. Like with someone else's *uncool* behavior. In those times, it's like a foghorn warning you to run—no need for intuition here.

Rather, intuition comes into play in times when you notice the little things, the little *knowings*, the little feelings that want to guide you. The problem is, we often ignore them. Or they're so small, you hardly notice them. Or your life is so "loud" that you can't hear your intuition speak. Or you talk "sense" into yourself, and ignore the hunch.

Describe a time when you had a gut feeling about something, and you were correct.

What Is Intuition Really?

Intuition is knowing something without conscious thought.

Arianna Huffington writes in her book, *Thrive*,

> *"Even when we're not at a fork in the road, wondering what to do and trying to hear that inner voice, our intuition is always there, always reading the situation, always trying to steer us the right way. But can we hear it? Are we paying attention? Are we living a life that keeps the pathway to our intuition unblocked? Feeding and nurturing our intuition, and living a life in which we can make use of its wisdom, is one key way to thrive, at work and in life."*

Can you be so in-tune with a situation that you develop an almost psychic ability to pick up on the smallest details? And just *know* what's going on? And what to do? And can you be mindful enough to pick up on these feelings? And listen to them?

Can you learn to *trust* your intuition?

The answer to all of these questions is yes. There's no magic to it. People have simply trained themselves to listen to their inner voice. They don't just have feelings, they ask themselves, *What are these feelings trying to tell me?*

And you can do this, too.

Paying attention to your intuition starts with recognizing its value, and then focusing on the *feeling* it creates inside you. You must quiet your mind, and let it really speak. It doesn't speak to you in words. It speaks in energy, in feelings.

But when our intuition is sending us signals, how can we make sure to listen?

How Can You Tap Into Your Intuition?

Here are some groovy tips for training yourself to listen to your golden intuition.

1. Set an Intuition Date

Set aside time every morning or evening for a 5-minute *intuition date*. Take this brief time in solitude to cultivate your intuition. This can be meditating or, quite literally, just staring at the wall. Notice how you feel, and then ask if that feeling is trying to tell you anything.

2. Get Creative

Make some art. Create something. Creating is often a great way to inspire intuition to come out and play. You can draw a picture, color, cook, paint, garden, knit... anything artistic that tickles your fancy.

3. Observe Details. Everywhere.

Wherever you go, make it a point to notice details. The details of a room you're in, the people you see, the things you see outside, or the things you hear, smell, etc. Notice where the light is coming from, and how it plays upon the surfaces. Paying attention to your senses helps you to become mindful, and when mindfulness becomes habit, your subconscious gets better at developing intuitive knowledge about all situations. It's like a muscle; if you exercise it, it will get stronger.

4. Go Get Some Nature

Exploring nature, even a simple walk through your neighborhood, where you focus on the birds, trees, grass, and sky, will help develop your intuition. If you ever get an opportunity to observe an artist or a photographer walking in nature, take note of the extreme attention they pay to the slightest details, which allows them to see things that others miss. You want to develop this kind of sensory superpower. But it's not magic, it's just simply paying attention to the world around you.

5. Journal Your Dreams

Keep a notebook by your bed. The next time you dream, immediatey upon waking, jot down as many details as you can recall. Do it right away—don't go pee first—or the memories will often fade quickly. But if you write them down, you'll remember them. Ask yourself what the dreams might mean. Especially objects... are they symbolic? Over time, see if there are any recurring symbols or common themes.

6. Listen to Your Body

Pay extra close attention to your energy, your cravings, and your feelings, especially minor shifts in mood, and try to identify what causes these shifts. As you do, you'll soon start to feel your intuition becoming more and more noticeable.

What I Love About Me

I am magnificent.

I am magical.

I am beyond.

On the first day of this journal, I asked you to write about what you love about your life.

Today, you're going to write about some of the things that you love about yourself. Feel free to repeat things you've written previously, or expand upon them, or write completely new things.

Your Turn to Shine!

What I love about me:

Logic vs. Creativity

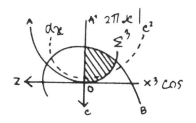

I have an unlimited supply of brilliant ideas,

creativity, and sparkling prosperity.

I'm a disciplined person. I set my mind to something, and I make a plan for how to attain it. Everything is very logical, a sequence of steps. I love making lists and schedules. I love organization.

When I was a child, I would write out a schedule detailing everything I would do to get ready in the morning before going to school. I wrote the schedule down to the minute:

7:00 AM   Wake up, get out of bed
7:05 AM   Brush teeth
7:07 AM   Get dressed
7:10 AM   And so on...

I was eight years old. It was cute, I'm sure.

Maybe a little crazy, too.

I carried this habit with me as I grew older, and it no doubt contributed to my success as a student, and as an employee, and a business owner.

But at some point, I realized I'd taken things too far. My compulsion and need for structure took a negative toll on my health and well-being. I was constantly operating in a state of high-beta, analytical brain waves. In this headspace, I was more comfortable swimming in spreadsheets than I was with a blank sheet of paper.

It wasn't until I read Dr. Joe Dispenza's book, *Becoming Supernatural*, that I saw so clearly how I was living my life *in a state of survival* with so many spreadsheets. My need to over-analyze things was based on *fear.*

And after loosening those reins—and understanding how they were negatively affecting me—I made some changes, and a whole new world opened up to me. A world filled with loving, calm energy, a world more Zen and chill. *A world full of creativity.* I discovered that, sometimes, having too much mental discipline can block your creativity.

That's because, when my brain wasn't stewing in high-beta brain waves, I had more opportunity to be in a state of *flow*, the result of *alpha* brain waves. Or to simply be relaxed, which meant I was open to ideas, and I was inspired. Instead of always relying on logic for making decisions, the more I opened to creative inspiration, the more I started living a magical life.

Logic Has a Home

Logic and spreadsheets have their place, but it's important to incorporate creativity in your life—even if you swear you don't have a creative bone in your body. In fact, the less creative you think you are, *the more you need it!*

It's time to open your mind to other sources of guidance. It's a bit like letting go... of control, and seeing where your unshackled mind takes you. Feel the incredible peace when you do this. If you find yourself starting to analyze again, say the word, *Swap! Swap! Swap!*, and swap brains right then and there, out loud, and clap your hands once with each word. Then swap out thoughts of logic for ones of creativity. It can be as simple as saying in that moment,

I am open to creativity.

And watch what happens.

I now intentionally *rely* more on creative inspiration for my magical life. I'm open to *Life's Flow*. It's real. It's a thing. And I tap into it. This was a big shift for me, and it didn't happen overnight, but I've arrived. As a result, I now always seem to have a ton more doors of sparkling opportunities all around. When I was stressed out with spreadsheets, I had blinders on, thinking myself in circles. Even if spreadsheets aren't your thing, do you know the feeling? Going round and round in your mind? Merry-go-rounds and dizziness. Rehashing the same problems but not seeing any solutions? Sometimes even feeling desperate, like you're trapped? Now that I'm open and in a state of mental flow, I'm always making more connections, having more peace, and manifesting my dreams faster.

Your Turn to Play!

Do you currently live primarily in a logical mental space or a creative mental space? Why? If it's a mix, describe the mix.

What feelings do you experience when you're in that space?

What time of day do you feel most creative? How do you take advantage of this?

_____

_____

_____

_____

What inspires you? What are some ways you can tap into your golden creativity?

_____

_____

_____

_____

What are your favorite ways to create?

_____

_____

_____

_____

When are your favorite times to be logical, or when does logical thinking seem to be most useful?

Is there anything you do regularly that combines logic and creativity? If so, describe how this works.

One Hundred Years

I am thankful for taking such great care

of myself and my body.

Describe yourself at 100 years of age, with details about your life and appearance.

_____

_____

_____

_____

_____

_____

Now, write a letter from 100-year-old you, to you at your current age today. What encouragement would you give? What loving thoughts and ideas would your future self impart to your present self? What anxieties might you have now that your future self would tell you to relax about? Are there interests you'd tell yourself to pursue? Are there any risks you would tell yourself that it's ok to take? Are there any regrets that your future self can tell you how to avoid?

Just One Goal

When I think big, my world gets bigger!

Today is a day to think about just one of your goals. One thing you want to manifest. It can be big or small, complex or simple. Whatever goal you pick, you'll make it the focus of this lesson.

Ok, got your goal?

(If not, pause here and think of something before proceeding.)

Write it here:

My One Goal ....

Now, close your eyes, and process the goal in your mind and heart by thinking positive things about it, imagining it realized, seeing the goal completed in your mind, and feeling elevated emotions that accompany how you'd feel accomplishing this.

Those two things—*thinking* the picture in your mind, and *feeling* the uplifted feelings— when combined, draw your dreams to you faster, and they make you happier because it feels good.

You see, your brain likes when you set goals. Your brain also likes every step you take toward attaining a goal, no matter how big or small the step. When you set goals, your brain secretes the happy neurotransmitter, dopamine, and it does so every step along the way. And this feels good, which keeps you motivated to take more steps toward your goal.

And remember, when our positive thoughts are in sync with our uplifted emotions, we attract and manifest faster. You take another little step toward your goal, and the dopamine drip repeats, and another step, another drip... and this cycle repeats until you reach your goal!

So, the trick is to start the process, to get the ball rolling. Let's put this all together for one big-ass manifesting party!

Your Turn to Shine!

Step 1: Thinking

Think about your goal. Close your eyes and picture yourself attaining this goal. How will attaining it change your life? In what ways will your life improve? Where are you physically located in this mental picture? What is happening around you when you attain this goal? Try to describe as many details as you can.

Step 2: Feeling

How will you feel when this goal is accomplished? Feel it in your heart... the awe, the love, the excitement you'll have. Feel it. Feel love now. Feel worthiness now. Write down as many sensations as you can.

_____

_____

_____

_____

_____

_____

_____

_____

Step 3: Surrender

Now let the dream go, by opening your hands and releasing it to the universe. This is a symbolic act, like you're placing your order with the universe. Your brain will notice, and start to work on making it happen, even when you're not thinking about it.

Step 4: Take Your First Steps

List three steps you can take right away to attain your goal. Do one of them today, and the other two over the next few days. For example, your goal might require researching and gathering information. Or scheduling an appointment. Or you might need to get organized and write out a plan. Perhaps you need to look at your finances or call someone to ask questions. And keep in mind, you're always free to change your goals as more information becomes available.

1. ....

2. ....

3. ....

Tell one person today about this goal. Write that person's name here. How will you tell them? In person? Via text or email? Facetime?

....

Think of someone whom you can ask for help with the goal, such as asking advice or gathering information, and write their name here.

....

Five People No Longer with Us

My ancestors were fighters, something I have inherited.

— Eric Cantona

Today, you'll be listing five people who are no longer living, and whom you've never met, but you wish you could've met while they were alive. The people on your list can be anyone you want, famous or not. Albert Einstein or your great-grandmother, it doesn't matter. The purpose of this activity is to get to know yourself better.

Your Turn to Shine!

Write your list of five dead people. (Assume they speak your language.)

Person #1

Why this person?

Questions you would ask this person:

Person #2

Why this person?

Questions you would ask this person:

Person #3

Why this person?

Questions you would ask this person:

Person #4

Why this person?

Questions you would ask this person:

Person #5

Why this person?

Questions you would ask this person:

Let's Get Bored!

The mind needs to wander and be bored.

Dreaming, after all, is a form of planning.

— Gloria Steinem

Boredom. Does it freak you out? If you grew up in the age of smartphones, the thought of spending twenty minutes in a waiting room without your phone might sound terrifying. Boredom is generally regarded as an unpleasant emotion because time seems to slow down. But boredom-time is a *powerful* time! And we need more boredom in our lives.

Why More Boredom?

In a fabulous TED Talk (*How Boredom Can Lead to Your Most Brilliant Ideas,* 2017), Manoush Zomorodi says,

"When you get bored, you ignite a network

in your brain called the default mode."

Why is this important? Because this default mode is a sort of autopilot for our brains. It's running the shop whenever you're spacing out, or doing repetitive tasks, etc. This is a good thing! During times like these, it may not seem like it, but your brain actually gets busy, triggering creativity. It allows for daydreaming, which is super *powerful,* and good for us, because it allows new and innovative connections to be made in our brains. At times like this, it's possible to realize things or discover new ideas that weren't likely to come to mind when we're actively focused on those topics. Daydreaming allows you to peek into the subconscious, and it lets you use your imagination to think in different ways.

In our Information Age, our brains are often overstimulated, so much that people panic if they're not constantly scrolling on their phone, getting notifications, etc. Too much FOMO (fear of missing out). But taking a break is a brilliant way to give your brain a break. A chance to let it relax. A chance to nurture creativity.

Sometimes, doing nothing can be your most important time. *Is it any wonder that some of the best ideas happen while taking a shower?*

Your Time to Shine!

What are the different ways you fill the gaps in your day? How many times do you pick up your phone *just because there's nothing else to do*? Pay attention to all the times you check email and social media. (Pro-tip: Occasionally leave your phone in another room, such as when it's charging.)

Make a list of some things you might think about—or daydream about—the next time you're "doing nothing."

_____

_____

_____

_____

_____

_____

_____

_____

_____

_____

Next, schedule time in your calendar, every day for the next week, to be bored, and *relish it*. Start with just five minutes at first. Stare at the wall, zone out, walk with nothing playing in your ears. Take five minutes and… do nothing. *Nothing. Nothing. Nothing.*

You might feel fidgety at first. That's ok, just keep doing it, and keep reminding yourself that you're not wasting time, you're *honoring yourself*. Then, next week, schedule ten minutes each day.

Give yourself permission to be bored, knowing how good it is for you. Be confident that it's going to help you live a more magical life. Eventually, the "boredom" will no longer feel boring, it will just feel like your special quiet time.

Happiness Day List

Creativity is easy for me to tap into,

and I see opportunities and solutions all around me.

Happiness is the ultimate medicine... *happiness helps you heal.* Happiness makes you feel good. Happiness helps make the world go round. So today, you'll start a list of all the things that make you happy.

Your Turn to Shine!

List things that make you happy. Here are some ideas to get you started: coffee, hugs, puppies, a good sleep, swimming, books, roses, music, stars at night, full moon...

For extra credit, write a note about why each one makes you happy.

Letting Go to Be

When I let go of who I am,

I become what I might be.

— Lao Tzu

Lao Tzu's words are profound. Transformation often means letting go of things, ways of living, behaviors... in order to become a new you.

If you long to become someone different, or to do something new, there are probably behaviors you're going to have to stop, or release. If you want to be someone who loves yourself more, then you need to stop criticizing yourself. If you desire to live a more relaxed, peaceful life, then you might need to let go of certain rules.

Your Turn to Shine!

What kind of person do you want to be?

....

....

....

....

....

What things (or behaviors) can you let go of now to be more like the person you want to be?

_____

_____

_____

_____

_____

_____

Longer term, what major changes would be required in you, or your thoughts, or behaviors, to fully transform into the person you'd like to become?

_____

_____

_____

_____

_____

Your "I'm Awesome" Résumé

My light shines so bright...

I am amazing. I am love. I am a shooting star!

It's time to sell yourself, baby.

Today, you're writing your *I'm Awesome* resume. As you're writing it, your job is to "go big or go home."

This is no time to be shy. Swing for the fence! You want to go nuts, writing every single thing that's amaze-balls about you!

It's much easier to sell someone on something *that you love*—like a great book, restaurant, movie, and so on—because you'll go on and on, gushing about how great it is. Well, how about selling someone on YOU because *you love you!*

It's time to go on and on about how wonderful, worthy, and loving you are. You are the whole incredible package, and now is your chance to list all the reasons you're so freakin' awesome.

List everything great about you, from your lustrous, sexy eyelashes, to your cute toes, to your quirky sense of humor, beautiful hair color, ability to parallel park, skill with flipping pancakes, or how cats instantly trust you. Can you beat anybody at beer pong, or juggle, or knit socks, or speak another language? Write it down.

In fact, once you get going, I'll bet you want to add even more because you are so friggin' amazing!

If you need some more questions to get the creative juices flowing, check these out:

- Got any numbers to back up your accomplishments? List them!

- Won any awards? List them all! (Even if you were five years old.)

- Do you have a big heart and love helping people?

- Are you generous?

- Do you have a great smile?

- Can you tie a cherry stem in a knot with your tongue?

- Did you win a spelling bee when you were eight years old?

- Did you ever work on any special projects?

- What are your strengths? Literally and figuratively. If you can bench press your own weight, then bravo!

- Do you work out twice a week or more?

- Do you make an amazing tuna salad sandwich?

- Can you speed read? Cook? Garden? Change a tire?

- Can you make people smile?

Whatever skills you have outright, or hiding somewhere inside, write them down on the following pages.

Your Turn to Shine!

Your Name: ....

Your Superhero Name: ....

I'm Awesome Because...

....

....

....

....

....

....

....

....

....

....

....

Clear the Cobwebs #2

I have clarity, and I think clearly every day. I love myself.

Today is a day for clearing out the cobwebs. Fill the following pages with anything that's been on your mind lately. Now you have a place to put it, and you don't need to think about it more, unless you want to.

There are no judgments, no right or wrong. No good or bad. Literally, you can write anything you want... your to-do list for the day or month, venting about anxieties, recalling your happiest memory, or a dream you had last night... anything that is in your mind as you write.

Doing this can be like a mini-therapy session, clearing the gunky cobwebs out of your brain, cleaning up, sweeping things out to give you a lovely, beautiful, and clear head for the rest of the day. Or, you may find that the writing process itself stimulates creativity, new thinking, and new ideas.

Whatever you start to write, just go with it, and see where it leads!

Self-Love List

I sparkle. I soar. I'm full of life. Swooooosh.

Self-love is essential to living a magical life.

The more you love yourself, the faster you attract your dreams, and the more amazing your life is in the process! Self-love *empowers* you. Self-love improves your health, boosts your happiness, and helps you grow into the fully actualized, beautiful person you're meant to be.

Make a list of all the things you love about yourself. Be specific and be general. Try to use up all of the lines! Use colored pens, draw hearts or stars or squiggly lines all over the page. Have fun. *This list is important!*

Note: This exercise is similar to writing your *I'm Awesome Résumé*, except this time, you're not selling yourself. You're appreciating all the reasons you have for loving yourself.

Once Upon a Time...

My life is bright and full of opportunities.

They are all around me, glittery and shiny.

It's fairytale time, and you're the author. Today, you get to tell a short story about you as the main character in a fairytale. Start with "Once upon a time," and make your main character (you) whatever age you like. In most good stories, the main character has an *arc*, meaning they are transformed somehow by the journey. Perhaps they learn something, or overcome a fear, or grow in some way. The character also needs a motivation or goal, and obstacles to overcome. If there are trials or villains in the tale, share how your character kicks butt, triumphing in the end, and living happily ever after in their magical life!

A few notes:

1. Your fairytale can be very short, so don't be intimidated if you've never written a story before. I've provided part of the first sentence to help you get started, but feel free to change it however you like.

2. The main character's name is your name.

3. The character's goal should be something you actually want in real life.

Your Turn to Shine!

Once upon a time, there was a _____ named _____

who wanted _____ ,

but she/he couldn't have it because

But then...

And she/he lived happily ever after.

Mining Memories

I have a powerful brain and memory.

I remember everything.

One of my favorite things to do is mine my memory for stories. As Joyce Carol Oates said,

"We are the stories we tell."

Stories are as old as culture. Hundreds of thousands of years before the invention of writing, people told stories around the campfire. It's believed that, in prehistoric times, the flickering light of the fire allowed people to unleash their imaginations and tell stories.

Stories served to both entertain and educate. We learn best when we learn through stories because stories help us understand the world. Other people's stories become examples of options and opportunities, and things to consider. Stories can even warn us of things not to do! When we tell stories, we share the lessons we've learned. When we hear stories, we get the chance to step into another person's shoes.

Storytelling connects us to people by hearing their stories and sharing ours. We bond.

Mining your own memory for stories is a powerful way to learn lessons about yourself, as well as inspire yourself. In fact, the same story, revisited at different times in your life, can have a different meaning each time. You can always find a gem of a lesson or inspiration when you go through your memory looking for stories.

Because storytelling is universal, if you're a writer (or a presenter), then mining your memory for material will enhance your creativity.

You can use your stories as ideas for characters, or as entertaining vignettes to tell when presenting at work, or as oral history to pass down to your children and grandchildren.

Your Turn to Shine!

Make a list of stories from your life. Go back as far in your memory as you can, and start at the earliest age you remember. Try to come up with at least one story per decade. Pro-tip: Play music from different periods of your life to help jog the memories. (Almost any song you can think of can be found for free on YouTube.)

Come up with a title for each memory, and then jot down a few notes about it. Later on, if you're feeling creative, choose one or more of them, and write it (or type it) as a complete story.

Title

Notes

Title

Notes

Title

Notes

Title

Notes

Title

Notes

Title

Notes

Eight Things I'd Like to Own

Everything I touch is a success.

I go from success, to success, to success.

Today, you get to go shopping in your mind!

And money is no object!

First, it's fun. Second, it's a bit like setting goals, or visualizing. There are no restrictions, so let your excitement be your guide. For example, an object can be a hot tub, or a house, or a leather jacket, or a drone, or even some fresh flowers on your dining room table.

This is a remarkable exercise because it's a great way to get to know yourself better, especially as you drill down into *why* you want certain things. You may discover some hidden gems that inspire new goals, hobbies, or passions. Or you might discover certain issues you want to work on.

Your Turn to Shine!

List eight items you would like to own. For each item, write at least two compelling reasons why you want it.

Item #1

Reasons

Item #2 ....

Reasons ....

....

Item #3 ....

Reasons ....

....

Item #4 ....

Reasons ....

....

Item #5 ....

Reasons ....

....

Item #6

Reasons

Item #7

Reasons

Item #8

Reasons

What If You Had Unlimited Time?

I have unlimited patience and generosity

because I have an abundance of time.

Today is a fun activity because you get to think about things you'd like to do *if you had all the time in the world.*

In my personal Coffee Self-Talk scripts, I often use the following line:

I have an abundance of time.

Every time I think it and say it, my shoulders relax, and a nice little wave of calm washes through me.

When I became an entrepreneur, I had a never-ending list of things to do. Everything was exciting, and I wanted to get everything done *right away...* every single, little thing could add dollars to my bottom line. But sometimes, I'd get tense thinking about a lack of time. Or I was impatient to get things done. Both of these are emotions rooted in scarcity, and ultimately, fear. They come from a sense of lack, a lack of time. And that kind of emotion does not attract abundance or help you live a magical life.

So today's activity is an exercise in visualizing having an abundance of time. You get to relish in the thoughts of all the things you'd get to do with unlimited free time!

During the whole time you're writing today, remember the following idea:

I have an abundance of time...

I have an abundance of time...

I have an abundance of time...

Your Turn to Shine!

Have fun answering the following questions! For more vibrance, flare, and emotional engagement, use colored pens or pencils to draw little pictures around the border of the page.

What five things will you do with your abundance of time?

Thing #1

Why?

Something I can do to do this activity more often:

Thing #2

Why?

Something I can do to do this activity more often:

Thing #3 ....

Why? ....

Something I can do to do this activity more often:

....

....

Thing #4 ....

Why? ....

Something I can do to do this activity more often:

....

....

Thing #5 ....

Why? ....

Something I can do to do this activity more often:

....

....

Going to Mars

What new possibilities exist that I will tap into and explore?

I see the possibilities.

In the previous exercise, you listed things you'd do if you had all the time in the world. In other words, if you had an abundance of time.

Today, you're going to think about the things you'd do *because you have a limited amount of time*, say, two months. Because, in two months, a Martian is coming down and taking you, and you alone, to Mars. You'll be comfy and safe on Mars, for the rest of your life, so don't worry about that part. There will be coffee, too.

But you'll never see Earth, or any other human again.

How would you spend your last two months here on Earth?

I don't normally think about things like *limited time*, but this is a solid exercise to help you focus on important things, and less on frivolous things, or wasting energy that can be better used elsewhere.

Your Time to Shine!

In the spaces that follow, list the top five things you would do during your two months before you leave Earth.

When you're done making your list, it's fascinating to compare it to your list of what you'd do if you had unlimited time!

Thing #1 ....

Why? ....

Something I can do to do this activity more often:

....

Thing #2 ....

Why? ....

Something I can do to do this activity more often:

....

Thing #3 ....

Why? ....

Something I can do to do this activity more often:

....

Thing #4 ....

Why? ....

Something I can do to do this activity more often:

....

Thing #5 ....

Why? ....

Something I can do to do this activity more often:

....

Magical Life Mission Statement

I am on a mission. I go out and do it.

I get things done!

What is a *Magical Life Mission Statement*?

This is a personal statement that defines 1) who you are, and 2) what your purpose is in your magical life. It can also explain how you aim to pursue that purpose, and why it matters so much to you.

When you write your Magical Life Mission Statement, three cool things happen:

1) You take a step back and look at the big picture, the grand design of your life. (If you don't know what that is yet, don't worry, I've provided some examples below that might inspire you.)

2) You get jazzed every time you read it. It's a great way to rise above the noise of daily life, and remind yourself why you're here, and what you're supposed to be working toward.

3) It helps create boundaries, which helps you make better decisions. Your mission statement serves as a roadmap for where you want to go in life. If something comes across your desk as an opportunity, you can run it by your Magical Life Mission Statement. If it fits, then great. But if it doesn't move you toward your dreams, then you can easily see this and pass on it. By saying no to distractions, you reach your dreams faster.

Tips for Writing Your Magical Life Mission Statement

Your Magical Life Mission Statement should be one to two sentences, and no more than about twenty-five words.

Focus on what really matters most to you.

Here are some examples:

"To be a teacher. And to be known for inspiring my students to be more than they thought they could be."

— Oprah Winfrey

"My mission in life is not merely to survive, but to thrive; and to do so with passion, compassion, some humor, and some style."

— Maya Angelou

"To use my smile to spread joy and inspire others to smile, too."

"To live my most epic life by always seeing the good in things."

"I write books to teach and delight children."

"To help women improve their self-worth, self-love, and wealth."

Your Turn to Shine!

Before writing your actual Magical Life Mission Statement, spend a few minutes writing down the things that are most important to you.

_____

_____

_____

_____

What would make your life more magical?

_____

_____

_____

_____

What do you want to accomplish?

_____

_____

_____

_____

What makes you shimmer and shine?

_____

_____

_____

_____

What fires you up and excites you to jump out of bed in the morning? If nothing currently does this, what _would_ make you?

_____

_____

_____

_____

Who all would benefit once you've successfully put this Magical Life Mission Statement into effect? List as many people as you can.

_____

_____

_____

_____

What are your core skills or superpowers that will help you attain the things you want to accomplish?

With the answers you provided above in mind, write some potential Magical Life Mission Statements, just to try them out and see how they feel.

From these statements, choose the one that makes you smile and stirs your soul the most. Make any final tweaks to it, and write it on the following page. You're always free to update your statement at any time.

For a free, 8.5" × 11" PDF of this that you can print out, color, and hang on your wall or refrigerator, email me at kristen@KristenHelmstetter.com — ask for the "Groovy Mission Statement PDF." *I HIGHLY recommend coloring this bad boy!* Doing so will engage your brain at all kinds of emotional and sensory levels, making it really stick!

Brain Blueprint: *I Am a...*

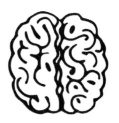

I stand in my own magnificent power.

Your mind talks to your body all day long with the words you use. Since your brain is always listening and waiting for instructions from you, today's exercise offers a way to keep those instructions front and center during the day, when you're not doing your *Coffee Self-Talk*.

Today, you're going to do a fun exercise using *Brain Blueprints*. Brain Blueprints are a powerful form of self-talk, using three words of description, in the form of:

I am a [adjective], [adjective] [noun].

Here are some examples:

I Am a Lean, Sexy Woman.

I Am a Smart, Driven Entrepreneur.

I Am a Kind, Generous Person.

Notice how these short phrases are short, to the point, and pack a punch? That's why they work so well. They're positive affirmations that catch your mind's attention, and direct it to helping you make it become true.

Basically, you're giving your brain a "blueprint," or a plan, from which to work in designing the life you want to live, and to transform you into the person you want to be.

You'll also notice that each one starts with the powerful words, *"I Am,"* and that's because the words that follow *I Am* define what you believe to be true about yourself or what you're going to become. When you begin a sentence with "I Am," you specify who and what you are, your life, and what you want to be.

Adjectives Galore!

There's a virtually unlimited number of adjectives you have to choose from, but here are just a few examples to get your creative juices going:

- Happy
- Sexy
- Intuitive
- Playful
- Confident
- Energetic
- Healthy
- Funny
- Loving

- Fertile
- Amazing
- Generous
- Fit
- Smart
- Friendly
- Passionate
- Prolific
- Lovable

- Calm
- Beautiful
- Clever
- Ambitious
- Strong
- Resourceful
- Determined
- Creative
- Wise

Nouns, Too!

And of course, there are many nouns from which to choose, too. Here are just a few examples:

- Woman/Man
- Wife/Husband
- Mom/Dad
- Millionaire
- Creator
- Investor
- Genius
- Artist
- Biohacker
- Writer
- Doctor
- Student
- Entrepreneur
- Teacher
- Friend
- Grandmother
- Engineer
- Inventor

From these, I can mix-n-match in all kinds of fun ways:

I Am a Happy, Sexy Millionaire

I Am a Sexy, Intuitive Woman

I Am a Funny, Happy Wife

I Am a Happy, Generous Friend

I Am a Funny, Loving Dad

I Am a Smart, Ambitious Entrepreneur

I Am a Healthy, Fertile Woman

I Am a Clever, Healthy Biohacker

You get the idea.

You mix them up, and come up with cool combinations.

Your Turn to Shine!

In the spaces below, write a mix of words of things you want to be... write them all over the place, like graffiti... don't write them in nice columns like I did, above. Write some of them crooked, some in different handwriting (print and cursive), maybe different colors, and start each word with a capital letter to distinguish it. The goal is to make a smattering of mixed-up words, like an artistic *word cloud*.

ADJECTIVES

NOUNS

Now, take three words and put them together. Do this ten times. You might even try choosing some words at random, by closing your eyes and pointing, just to see what happens.

Write the combinations here:

I Am a _____ _____ _____ .

I Am a _____ _____ _____ .

I Am a _____ _____ _____ .

I Am a _____ _____ _____ .

I Am a _____ _____ _____ .

I Am a _____ _____ _____ .

I Am a _____ _____ _____ .

I Am a _____ _____ _____ .

I Am a _____ _____ _____ .

I Am a _____ _____ _____ .

Next, read through the list three times. Out loud, if possible.

Finally, read the list three times, again, before you fall asleep tonight. Again, out loud, if possible.

Self-Love List #2

I believe in the power of my mind so hard

that I feel it in my bones,

my soul shimmers, and I glow with radiant purpose.

As I wrote earlier in this journal, self-love is *vital* to living a magical life. The more you love yourself, the faster you attract your dreams, and the more amazing your life is in the process. That is why you're making another Self-Love List for today's exercise.

Organizing your thoughts around the activities that make you feel happy and whole will encourage you to set aside special time for yourself, and it will help you tap into an amazing source of inner power.

This list will be a bit different, in that I'll ask you a series of questions to answer. And because all the things you'll think about while writing this list are things you love, you'll have more ideas for how to *give yourself* more self-love.

Your Turn to Shine!

Answer the following questions, and then show yourself some self-love by making a plan to enjoy some of them sometime during the next seven days!

Ok, let's begin...

What are two of your favorite leisure activities?

Leisure activity #1 ....

Why do you like it?

....

....

Leisure activity #2 ....

Why do you like it?

....

....

What is one of your favorite foods? ....

Why do you like it?

....

....

What are your favorite TV shows?

Why do you like them?

What are your favorite kinds of books?

Why do you like them?

What are your favorite kinds of music or bands?

Why do you like them?

What are your favorite places to travel?

Why do you like them?

Who are two of your favorite people to spend time with?

Person #1

Why do you like them?

Person #2

Why do you like them?

Focusing on Others

I love meeting new people and sharing ideas.

I love listening to others and learning.

Getting out of yourself and focusing on others is a great way to spread love and, ironically, increase feelings of love *inside* you. *We are one.*

Sometimes when you get frustrated, or your creativity is blocked, or you're just feeling a little "off," the best thing you can do is to leave yourself for a bit, and set off to help others.

Why do this?

Because it helps others, sure. But guess what? It also helps *you!*

Helping others promotes self-compassion, which makes you shimmer and shine. It decreases stress and anxiety, and makes you feel all gooey and good. When you help others, your brain thinks, "I have an abundance of resources." And guess what? Your brain makes it happen!

How can you tap into this awesomeness? Many ways!

Helping others can be as simple as holding them in your mind and feeling how much you love them. It can be sending an encouraging text message or email, or a letter or card in the mail. It can be a phone call. It can be asking someone, *"What can I do to help you today?"*

Another powerful and proven way is through a Buddhist practice called *Metta* meditation. This typically involves repeating just four lines. It starts with sending love toward yourself, then to someone you know, then to someone you don't know personally but you know of, and then to the world.

Here's the script:

> *May I be loved.*
>
> *May I be safe.*
>
> *May I be happy.*
>
> *May I have peace.*

Then, you say it for someone you know. As you think of the person, say (or think):

> *May you be loved.*
>
> *May you be safe.*
>
> *May you be happy.*
>
> *May you have peace.*

Then, you think of someone you don't know personally, and repeat it. This is especially effective to do toward someone you don't particularly resonate with, such as a politician. It's a powerful way of letting go of negative emotions, which are only harming you when you hold onto them.

And finally, repeat the same lines for all beings in the world.

Your Turn to Shine!

List ten things you can do to help people in some way. If it's someone you know, include their name.

1. ....

2. ....

3. ....

4. ....

5. ....

6. ....

7. ....

8. ....

9. ....

10. ....

Five Things Calm People Do

I feel an ocean wave of peace wash over me.

What do you think living a calm, peaceful life would be like?

Would you like to be calmer and more relaxed? Would you like to be more chill and go with the flow?

What would it do for you? What do you think about people who exude a calm and chill vibe? What does that person do that makes them seem so relaxed? How do they act? What do they look like?

One way to reduce stress and anxiety is to have a calmer mind. And to help you attain that state, your task is to think of how a calm person thinks and behaves. What do calm people do?

By thinking about these things, you'll have a person to model yourself after. You'll have social proof that such a persistent state of mind is indeed possible, and you'll discover new ways to bring more calmness into your life.

Your Turn to Shine!

Make a list of five things a calm person does. How does that person look? What expression do they have on their face? What activities do you expect them to do? How do they stand and walk? What are the habits of calm people? Do they listen to certain types of music? Do they read certain types of books? Do they exercise or focus on gratitude? How do they react to things they didn't expect?

If you can think of more than five, then by all means, keep adding to the list!

1. ....

2. ....

3. ....

4. ....

5. ....

After you've written your list, pick one or two of the items, and write down what you can do to behave this way more often.

....

....

....

....

....

....

....

....

Childhood Influences

I am love. I am wonder. I am everything good.

Much of who we are today stems from our childhood and the people, events, and inspirations we experienced, saw, heard, and read. Thinking about these influences can give you insight into your life today, and who you are as a person.

You might even have an "a-ha" moment, especially if you've never really thought much about your influences. Or you might remember something comical... like those things that make you say, "We'll laugh about this one day."

Whatever the influences you recall now, consider whether they were positive or negative in their effect on you.

Your Turn to Shine!

What are some books that influenced you as a child? Go back as far in your memory as you can. What effect did they have on you?

_____

_____

_____

_____

_____

What TV shows or movies had an impact, and what was that impact?

What person had a major impact on who you are today? How did he or she influence your life? Is their effect on you serving the current you in a positive way? If not, how might you change the way he or she influences you going forward?

What is an event that had a major impact on who you are today? How did it influence your life?

Is the effect of this event on you serving the current you in a positive way? If not, how might you change the way it influences you going forward?

Childhood Exploring

My innate curiosity about the world

fills me with wonder and awe every day.

In the spaces below, answer the following questions about your childhood.

What were you like as a kid?

What are three traits about yourself as a child that you admire, and why?

Trait #1

Trait #2

Trait #3

Were you ever scared of anything as a child? If so, what was it, and how do you feel about that thing now?

List some of your favorite memories from childhood.

Pick one of these memories, and describe it in as much detail as possible. Also describe why you're so fond of it.

Clear the Cobwebs #3

I am magnificent. I am lovable. I approve of myself.

Today is a day for clearing out the cobwebs. Fill the following pages with anything that's been on your mind lately. Now you have a place to put it, and you don't need to think about it more, unless you want to.

There are no judgments, no right or wrong. No good or bad. Literally, you can write anything you want... your to-do list for the day or month, venting about anxieties, recalling your happiest memory, or a dream you had last night... anything that is in your mind as you write.

Doing this can be like a mini-therapy session, clearing the gunky cobwebs out of your brain, cleaning up, sweeping things out to give you a lovely, beautiful, and clear head for the rest of the day. Or, you may find that the writing process itself stimulates creativity, new thinking, and new ideas.

Whatever you start to write, just go with it, and see where it leads!

Super Fun Cleaning Day

I sparkle, shimmer, and shine!

Having a clean slate is refreshing. It's an opportunity to start over. And that mindset is powerful for clearing the decks for creativity, and thinking in general. Today's activity is to pick something you want to clean or declutter in your life. You'll set a 22-minute timer to do it. (Why 22? To make it stand out, and being less than 25 makes it seem so doable.)

The activity is not only about improving your physical space and clearing your mind. It's also an opportunity to draw your magical life closer to you using positive affirmations. The other thing you're going to do while cleaning or decluttering is picking out a line from your *Coffee Self-Talk*, either short or long, and repeating it the whole time you're doing the activity, mantra style.

Alternatively, if you've made one, you could listen to a recorded copy of your Coffee Self-Talk script. (Or listen to the free one I sent to you as a reader of the book, *Coffee Self-Talk*, if you've requested it.)

Note: If you haven't read Coffee Self-Talk, here are some examples to choose from:

I am a magnificent person.

I am love.

I am powerful.

Abundant wealth is coming to me.

I am beautiful.

Tip: Prior to doing this cleaning and decluttering activity, you can get yourself into the mindset to actually be *excited about it*. Excited about cleaning and decluttering? Yes! Whether it's vacuuming your house or organizing drawers, you can look forward to it by simply saying, "I love <insert activity>!" I know... it's wacky, but it works.

For example, if I'm going to organize the shelves in my garage, I'd say, "I love cleaning my garage!" I'd say it as I'm planning it beforehand, and I'd say it as I'm walking to the garage. And the weird thing is that it actually makes the whole project more enticing. The mind is amazing like that, and it'll listen to what you tell it. If you tell it you love something, then, in that moment, it can't not love it. This even works for doing taxes!

Here is a list of things to consider doing for your *Super Fun Cleaning Day*:

- Refrigerator

- Garage

- Car

- Junk drawer

- Closet

- Desk

- Laundry room

- Vacuum or mop the floor

- Under the bed

- Your computer's desktop

Decide what you're going to work on, and write it here:

How will your life be better once it's done?

How do you think you'll feel once it's done?

Magical Life Playlist

Music makes me feel wonderful and lets my spirit soar!

Today, you're going to make a music score for your life.

A soundtrack to live by!

Music is one of the easiest ways to elevate your emotions. Research has shown that people who intentionally listened to upbeat music improved their moods and happiness in just two weeks. I find that music affects me instantly. It's a powerful tool for changing your state.

The more you listen to uplifting music, the more often you'll feel uplifted! It gives you energy and puts you in an empowered state where you can feel *unlimited*. These are the feelings you want to tap into regularly throughout the day to keep manifesting and living your legendary life.

Your Turn to Shine!

Create a *Magical Life Playlist* on your smartphone or computer, where every song on it immediately puts you into an awesomely elevated state. You know, like the songs that make you want to dance, or drop to your knees in gratitude, or strike a superhero power-pose, or fly your golden dragon into battle! You know the ones!

The first step is to list a bunch of possible candidate songs, and indicate how each one makes you feel. Then, curate your playlist (or multiple playlists) by grouping 10-20 songs by similar emotional states, or themes, or perhaps in some narrative that moves through several different emotions.

The emotions you indicate on your list might include words like:

- Inspired
- Awe
- Invigorated
- Alive
- Excited
- Ecstatic
- Calm
- Relaxed
- Happy

- Sexy
- Vivacious
- Determined
- Resilient
- Strong
- Bold
- Courageous
- Wild
- Playful

- Confident
- Intuitive
- Energetic
- Healthy
- Ambitious
- Resourceful
- Peaceful
- Creative
- Bliss

... and so on.

If you create multiple playlists, give each playlist a special name that resonates with you personally, and matches the mood you intend to create. It could be something symbolic, that only you would understand.

And then, make sure that one of your playlists is extra special... the *master playlist*, if you will. This one will be the soundtrack, or score, for this time in your life. It will be your go-to music, whenever you want to create an immediate *Magical Life* mindset.

Song .... Makes me feel ....

Song .... Makes me feel ....

Song .... Makes me feel ....

Song .... Makes me feel ....

Song .... Makes me feel ....

Song .... Makes me feel ....

Song .... Makes me feel ....

Song .... Makes me feel ....

Song .... Makes me feel ....

Song .... Makes me feel ....

Song .... Makes me feel ....

Song .... Makes me feel ....

Song .... Makes me feel ....

Song .... Makes me feel ....

Song .... Makes me feel ....

Song .... Makes me feel ....

Song .... Makes me feel ....

Song ....   Makes me feel ....

Song ....   Makes me feel ....

Song ....   Makes me feel ....

Song ....   Makes me feel ....

Song ....   Makes me feel ....

Song ....   Makes me feel ....

Song ....   Makes me feel ....

Song ....   Makes me feel ....

Song ....   Makes me feel ....

Song ....   Makes me feel ....

Song ....   Makes me feel ....

Song ....   Makes me feel ....

Song ....   Makes me feel ....

Song ....   Makes me feel ....

Song ....   Makes me feel ....

Song ....   Makes me feel ....

My Magical Life Playlist

I want to see your list! Take a picture of your playlist, and post it to our amazing Facebook group:

facebook.com/groups/coffeeselftalk

Finding Things to Like in People You Don't Like

I am on a mission to be the best person I can be.

Today is a powerful exercise for improving your life.

This cool activity will help make your life more magical because it's going to assist you in drawing your dreams and goals to you faster. As I detailed in the book, *Coffee Self-Talk*, the key elements to manifesting include *thinking* about your dream life and *feeling* elevated emotions at the same time.

When your thoughts and feelings are in sync, you overcome any internal resistance or self-doubt, and that's when the magic happens. It's the *thinking plus the feeling* that helps you create the positive energy that allows you to take actions and draw your magical life to you faster.

Not to mention, it feels fantastic in the moment, which will make you happy.

With this in mind, today you're going to apply uplifted emotions to something you don't usually associate with good feelings: *people who aren't your jam.*

Specifically, you're going to train yourself to be happier when you think about these people and when you spend time around them.

Why?

It'll give you less stress, less negativity, and it'll increase your happy thoughts and feelings.

Your Turn to Shine!

Ready? Let's go!

Think about somebody that, shall we say... you're not always in love with. (I'm putting it as kindly as I can.) Or maybe someone you feel neutral about, but whom you'd like to feel better toward. Pick three of these people. They can be people you know... that's best. But if you already absolutely adore everyone around you (lucky you!), then pick a person you don't know, but you, however, don't like very much. Maybe a politician?

Write their names in the spaces on the following page.

After each person's name, write one to three positive things about that person. If you find this difficult at first, it's probably because you're focused on their negative traits, as these are the most relevant to you on any given day. But even people who are hard to get along with usually have some redeeming qualities. Perhaps they're skilled at something, or they're nice to animals. Or maybe they're very smart, if only in an evil-genius kind of way.

The more positive things you can come up with, the better it will be for you, because it'll help dilute your negative emotions toward this person. It could be their organizational skills, their ability to change a tire, their smile, their eyelashes, or their shoes. Start somewhere, and build from there.

I'm not suggesting you instantly start liking the person, only that you try to have an open mind about their good qualities. It's a more mature and nuanced way of thinking about others, and the main beneficiary is you, as you make your way through life with less negativity.

If you make this your habit, you'll soon discover that troublesome people simply don't bother you as much as they used to. That's the goal.

Person #1

    Good quality

    Good quality

    Good quality

Person #2

    Good quality

    Good quality

    Good quality

Person #3

    Good quality

    Good quality

    Good quality

Twenty Things Healthy People Do

I am strong and confident.

I like being healthy.

When you're making a plan and attracting a goal or desire, it helps to have a clear picture of precisely what that goal is. Many people have a desire or goal to have a healthy body, and this exercise will help make that happen. If you're already healthy, it will inspire you that much more.

Your Turn to Shine!

Make a list of things that healthy people do, such as their habits, activities, exercise, eating, odd quirks, and so on. For instance, healthy people deliberately park farther from the store entrance. They take the stairs instead of the elevator. They floss their teeth.

Also, include in your list answers to questions such as, What does a healthy person look like? How do they stand and walk? What kind of glow do they have? How lustrous is their hair?

Aim for 20 items on your list.

After you write your list, pick one or two of the things that healthy people do (that you don't currently do), and add them to your Coffee Self-Talk script or daily to-do list.

Over the next couple of weeks, try to make them a new, regular habit.

Twenty things healthy people do:

1.	11.
2.	12.
3.	13.
4.	14.
5.	15.
6.	16.
7.	17.
8.	18.
9.	19.
10.	20.

Magical Life Community

I am lovable. So very, very lovable.

And I have love to give.

Having people around you who support the idea of *you attracting your dreams and goals* can *greatly* enhance your magical life.

And, of course, people who resist the idea can slow you down.

When you have trusted people with whom you can share your dreams (and when you support their dreams, too), it becomes both a teaching and a learning opportunity. These connections keep the happiness drip dripping, and it keeps the elevated emotions alive, in the center of your mind's awareness.

If you don't have anyone you can turn to, then it's time to go find them!

One way to find like-minded souls is to join our private Coffee Self-Talk Facebook group (facebook.com/groups/coffeeselftalk), which is full of incredible folks who love supporting each other, sharing their progress in attaining goals, and living their magical lives.

Another idea is to go to Meetup.com and create your own local "Coffee Self-Talk" meetup group. *How fun!*

Or start a book club, or a Coffee Self-Talk discussion group (write to me at kristen@ KristenHelmstetter.com for a free CST Discussion Guide). Or simply set up a weekly coffee, even if it's just you and one other person. Or a weekly Zoom chat. It's powerful!

For me, I have a couple of good girlfriends who love doing things like Coffee Self-Talk, reading personal development books, and constantly finding ways to enhance our lives.

(My mom, husband, daughter, and brother are great for this, too!) We love chatting about ways to live a magical life. We pump each other up and encourage each other. If one of us has an off day, then the other one is there to cheer us on.

Before we sold all of our stuff to travel the world, when we lived in Scottsdale, Arizona, my husband and his high school buddy used to meet every other Friday afternoon for coffee. They divided the allotted time into two halves, spending the first half focusing on just one of them, and then switching to the other person during the second half of the meeting. They would each talk about what they were working on, (whether work-related or personal), and any updates, plans, or progress they had made toward their goals since the last time they met.

They provided each other with not only support, ideas, and feedback, but also with mutual accountability and inspiration.

Having someone you can regularly talk to about your goals, plans, and progress is an incredibly powerful way to accelerate your magical life.

Do you have someone like this you can talk to? Or multiple people? If not, it's time to find someone!

Your Turn to Shine!

Make a list of people that you do, or could, regularly meet with to accelerate your magical life. If you don't know anybody who fits the bill, then list the steps you can take to build this kind of "mastermind" community... or even just one great person!

People I know who might be interested in being a member of my Magical Life
community:

Steps I can take to find more like-minded people:

What Matters to You?

I am aligned with my goals and beautiful desires.

About three years into my marriage, my husband and I were doing our annual New Year's Eve ritual of reviewing what we had accomplished the previous year and writing down our goals for the new year to come.

In previous years, for this exercise, I used to divide a piece of paper into different facets of my life: health, career, relationships, financial, spiritual, leisure, and the like. I would draw a grid, get my colored pens—*of course*—and then I would list different goals under each category for the year.

Well, when I came to the relationships section that year, I thought... I'd like to take my relationship with my husband even deeper, by finding out what *really* matters to him, and figuring out how I can support that.

We'd been together for five years... you'd think I would already know that, right? Well, yes, kinda sorta... but had I ever actually asked him?

So I turned to him and asked, "For our relationship, and our marriage, and our life going forward together, what matters to you?"

Notice... I didn't ask him what it was that he "wanted," per se. No, that is a different kind of question. Asking him *what matters* probes deeper. It's about core values. Priorities.

Well, we had an incredible conversation from that one simple question. He gave me an answer I didn't expect! And then we talked about ways to make what mattered to him a priority in our life. And then we flipped it, and I told him what mattered to me. In this way, we could support each other.

Your Turn to Shine!

Take this opportunity to answer the question for yourself. What matters to you in life? Is it global peace? Helping animals? Is it health and longevity? Succeeding through goals? Seeing your children succeed? Seeing them happy?

Write the top five things that matter most to you. They don't have to be in order of importance, but if you know, then go ahead and rank them. You might be tempted to keep adding more than five items, but the purpose of this exercise is not to identify *everything* that's important to you, but what's *most* important.

Beneath each item, write why it matters to you. Go deep, and let it all rip. Let the words flow out of you, and keep going until you fill the space.

1. What matters to you?

Why?

2. What matters to you? _____

Why?

_____

_____

_____

_____

3. What matters to you? _____

Why?

_____

_____

_____

_____

4. What matters to you? ....

Why?

....

....

....

5. What matters to you? ....

Why?

....

....

....

Well done!

But wait, there's more...

What are ten ways that you can start doing more in your life to support these five things that matter to you?

1. ....

2. ....

3. ....

4. ....

5. ....

6. ....

7. ....

8. ....

9. ....

10. ....

Mad Skillz

I am the master conductor of the amazing life I'm designing.

There's something very satisfying about acquiring a new skill.

Learning a new skill makes us feel accomplished, reminds us that we're capable of learning new things, regardless of age (which is true), and in some cases, the skill might enhance our ability to succeed, such as by making us more marketable on the job market, or simply allowing us to do things ourselves without hiring somebody to do them for us.

I'll share a secret with you... here's what's on my Mad Skillz horizon: archery, Brazilian Jiu-Jitsu, coding, poetry, and proficiency in Italian, Spanish, and Portuguese. Will I master all of these? I don't know. The important thing is that I'm always *working toward* mastering some new skill.

Your Time to Shine!

What are five things that you would like to be good at?

Skill #1 ....

Why would you like to get good at this?

....

....

....

Skill #2

Why would you like to get good at this?

Skill #3

Why would you like to get good at this?

Skill #4

Why would you like to get good at this?

Skill #5 _____

Why would you like to get good at this?

_____

_____

_____

Would acquiring one of these skills be a better use of your free time than whatever you are currently doing? Why or why not?

_____

_____

_____

What are three steps (even tiny steps) you could take to start developing this skill?

1. _____

2. _____

3. _____

Bucket List

I make the most of every day of my life.

While some people find thoughts of our mortality to be negative or gloomy, others flip it around, using the knowledge to motivate them to take action and not waste their lives. As time ticks by and the birthdays add up, it's a good idea to periodically revisit your "bucket list," or list of things you want to do before you kick the bucket.

What are ten things that you intend to do before you die?

1. _____

2. _____

3. _____

4. _____

5. _____

6. _____

7. _____

8. _____

9. _____

10. _____

Now choose the most important three items that you just wrote down, and explain why they are important to you.

Bucket List Item #1 ....

Why is it important to you?

....

....

....

Bucket List Item #2 ....

Why is it important to you?

....

....

....

Bucket List Item #3 ....

Why is it important to you?

....

....

....

Conclusion

Well!

Congratulations on reaching the end... I feel like I've been with you on the journey!

If you haven't already done so, please check out our private Facebook group... it's an amazing group!

facebook.com/groups/coffeeselftalk

And don't forget... for a free, 8.5" × 11" PDF of the *Magical Life Mission Statement* form that you can print out, color, and hang on your wall or refrigerator, email me at:

kristen@KristenHelmstetter.com

Ask for the "Groovy Mission Statement PDF." *I HIGHLY recommend coloring this,* to make it really stick in your brain and give you joy and motivation every time you see it!

And finally, I have a HUGE favor to ask of you.

If you would help me, I'd greatly appreciate it. I'd love it if you would leave a review for this *Coffee Self-Talk Guided Journal* on Amazon (even if you bought it somewhere else). Reviews are incredibly important for authors, and I'm extremely grateful if you would write one!

What's Next?

Here are a few more members of the Coffee Self-Talk family:

  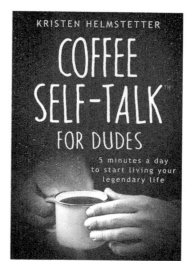

Coffee Self-Talk

This is the original book, and it explains what Coffee Self-Talk is, and how and why to do it. The book teaches you how to create your own Coffee Self-Talk scripts and provides a wide range of sample scripts to get you started.

The Coffee Self-Talk Daily Reader #1

This is a supplemental companion to the original *Coffee Self-Talk*, for people who would like to add a little extra magic to their daily ritual. It offers short, daily reads for tips and inspiration. It's meant to be used each day after you do your Coffee Self-Talk. If you do one reading per day, it will take 30 days to complete.

The Coffee Self-Talk Blank Journal (and Teen Girls Blank Journal)

These are exactly that: blank journals (with lines). There are no words, except for a one-page intro. These journals provide a place to write your own scripts, as well as journal your thoughts and progress. You could use any notebook, but readers asked for matching journals to make things fun and help reinforce their daily Coffee Self-Talk ritual.

Coffee Self-Talk for Teen Girls

This book is for girls in high school (ages 13 to 17 years old). It covers the same ideas as *Coffee Self-Talk*, and applies them to the issues that teen girls face, such as school, grades, sports, peer pressure, social media, social anxiety, beauty/body issues, and dating.

Coffee Self-Talk for Dudes

This is a special edition of *Coffee Self-Talk* that has been edited to be more oriented toward men. It is 95% identical to the original book.

Printed in Great Britain
by Amazon